THE CRACKER BOOK

THE CRACKER BOOK

LEE E. CART

Illustrations by Joan Cart

Bb

BURFORD BOOKS

Printed in the United States of America.

10 9 8 7 6 5 4 3 2 1

Library of Congress Cataloging-in-Publication Data
is on file with the Library of Congress.

For Jeffrey, with lots of love
and to Bruce Kliewer, as promised

CONTENTS

INTRODUCTION

W E'VE ALL HEARD IT A HUNDRED TIMES. Trans fats are bad for you; trans fats increase your risk of heart attacks. Trans fats lower your good cholesterol and raise your bad cholesterol. Do not eat trans fats. And yet those pesky fats are in some of the foods most people eat on a regular basis with chunks of cheese, or with slices of ham or pepperoni. Yup, trans fats are in many of the brands of crackers we all enjoy daily. So what can you do to avoid those bad saturated fats and still enjoy peanut butter and crackers as an afternoon snack? Why, make your own healthy crackers from scratch right at home, using canola oil and olive oil. These two are among the most heart-healthy oils on the market. No more hydrogenated vegetable oils or saturated stick-to-your-arteries fats, but simple mono–unsaturated fats that are easy to digest and actually good for you.

Making crackers isn't difficult and doesn't require a lot of fancy equipment. If you have an oven, a cookie sheet, a mixing bowl, a mixing spoon, and a rolling pin, with a few simple ingredients you can be making heart-healthy, tasty crackers for your family in about thirty minutes. Try serving Barbecue Crackers, Cheddar Cheese Crackers, and Tomato and Basil Crackers at your next football party. Or Curry and Brown Rice Crackers, Black Pepper and Rye Crackers, and Salsa and Cornmeal Crackers to those who love it on the spicy side.

With the following recipes, not only will you be creating healthy alternatives to store-bought crackers for yourself and your family, but you'll also have the fun of creating them in whatever shapes you want. Pull out those cookie cutters that are used only once or twice a year! Make stars, clovers, diamonds, trees, chickens, whatever shapes you want, all the time knowing that you are creating tasty and healthy treats for the ones you love.

And once you learn the basic recipe, you are only limited by your own imagination as to what those crackers might taste like. So break out a few ingredients, turn on the oven, and let's get baking heart-healthy crackers!

A BRIEF HISTORY OF THE CRACKER

WHO REALLY INVENTED THE CRACKER? In 1792 Theodore Pearson of Newburyport, Massachusetts, owned Pearson and Sons Bakery. He combined flour and water into a hardtack he called Pearson's Pilot Bread. Because of its long shelf life, the pilot cracker became a great favorite with sailors, who relied on it for sustenance on long sea voyages. This type of cracker was manufactured in the United States until 2008.

The prototype of today's modern cracker came about by accident. According to stories, in 1801 Josiah Bent of Massachusetts, owner of the Josiah Bent Bakery, left a batch of biscuits in the oven just a little too long, and they began to "crackle." Bent played with the recipe and came up with a snack food that sold like hotcakes. In 1889 Bent sold his bakery to William Moore. Moore acquired six other bakeries and started the New York Biscuit Company. In 1890 Adolphus Green obtained forty different bakeries and started the American Biscuit & Manufacturing Company. These two large bakery firms converged in 1898, becoming the National Biscuit Company, whose name later was shortened to Nabisco. Now part of Kraft Foods, Inc., Nabisco is still a leading manufacturer of crackers in the United States.

INGREDIENTS

FLOURS

Unbleached all-purpose flour: I use King Arthur Unbleached All-Purpose Flour as the basic flour in all these recipes. Milled from the heart or endosperm of hard red winter wheat grown in Kansas, this flour is high in gluten and rich in flavor yet light and airy, too.

Whole wheat flour: Milled from all three parts of the wheat berry—the endosperm, the germ, and the bran—this flour contains many valuable nutrients as well as fiber. It should be stored in the refrigerator or in a cool place, so the natural oils in it do not turn rancid. Rancid flour tastes bitter—if your flour tastes bitter, replace it with a fresh bag. Whole wheat flour should taste sweet and slightly nutty.

Brown rice flour: Finely milled from brown rice, this flour has no gluten, so it needs to be mixed with all-purpose to produce a dough that is soft and easier to roll. It adds a slightly crunchy texture to crackers as well as a nutty flavor.

Cornmeal: Ground from whole yellow corn, finely ground meal works the best in these recipes. Corn contains no gluten, so this flour needs to be used in combination with all-purpose to make stretchable dough. These crackers call for yellow cornmeal, but feel free to substitute blue cornmeal, taking into account the shift in flavors, different colors, and slight texture differences.

Dark rye flour: Rye is available in light or dark flours; dark rye has a deeper, richer flavor and produces a darker-colored cracker. Rye has a good gluten content, but produces a much stickier dough than all-purpose, so this flour needs to be blended with all-purpose to allow ease in rolling.

Millet flour: Low in gluten and high in protein, millet flour is gritty in texture, so it needs to be used in moderation in these recipes. Combine it with all-purpose or whole wheat to make a dough that rolls easily.

Buckwheat flour: This flour has a distinctive, almost earthy taste, one you either love or hate. Like most flours milled from the whole kernel, buckwheat can turn rancid quickly, so store this flour in the refrigerator or in a cool place. If the flour is bitter, be sure to replace it with a fresh bag before beginning to bake. Because it has such a strong flavor, use small amounts of this flour in these recipes.

Graham flour: Slightly coarser in texture than regular whole wheat due to the milling process, graham flour is named for the Reverend Sylvester Graham of Massachusetts, who advocated for the inclusion of bran in foods to promote good health. A slightly more textured flour, graham adds a sweet, nutty taste to crackers and has a slightly longer shelf life than regular whole wheat flour.

Rolled oats: Regular whole oats contain little gluten and need to be mixed with all-purpose or whole wheat flours to produce a stretchy dough suitable for rolling. Oats add a mild flavor and crunchy texture to crackers and look good sprinkled on top as well as mixed into a dough.

Pecan meal: Finely ground pecans make up this soft, powdery flour. Made of nuts, this flour will quickly turn rancid if left at room temperature, so be sure to purchase and store small quantities only or grind your own as needed.

OILS

Canola oil: Pressed from the canola seed, which is similar to rapeseed, canola oil is low in saturated fats and high in monounsaturated fats, and contains beneficial omega-3 fatty acids. Canola oil has been declared a heart-healthy oil by the U.S. Food and Drug Administration because of its ability to help reduce the risk of coronary heart disease. Various forms of canola oil are available, from organic to expeller-pressed to refined. Buy the best oil you can afford and check it frequently to make sure it is not rancid. Oils, like flours, can turn quickly and will taste bitter when they have gone by. Store canola oil in a cool, dark place to protect its flavor and shelf life.

Olive oil: Pressed from olives, olive oil is high in monounsaturated fats. The U.S. Food and Drug Administration states that olive oil also has the ability to reduce the risk of coronary heart disease. For these recipes, I recommend a virgin or extra-virgin olive oil, preferably organic. The richer flavor and lighter color will produce a better cracker. Olive oil is light yellowish green in color with a slightly strong taste to it, so experiment with different brands until you find one you like. Olive oil should be sweet to the taste; if it's bitter, throw it out. If possible, store olive oil in the refrigerator; if this is not possible, then keep it in a cool, dark place to protect its flavor and shelf life.

Note: To ensure the best-tasting crackers, buy the highest-quality oils available in your area. The best are organic, expeller-pressed canola oils and extra-virgin olive oils that you keep in a cool place or store in the refrigerator. Check the flavor of the oil; if it is at all bitter, throw it out and buy a new bottle. Bitter oil has turned rancid and should not be used.

A WORD ABOUT SHAPES

ALL THE CRACKERS IN THIS BOOK were made using a two-inch round biscuit cutter as a shape. This was to make it easier to compute the number of crackers each recipe makes. However, please feel free to experiment with other shapes, like squares, triangles, clovers, and so on. Break out the cookie cutters and make caraway-rye men instead of gingerbread men for Christmas, cheddar cheese stars, lemony-dill ducks, tomato-basil turkeys, or whatever shape cutters you happen to have. You are only limited by your imagination! Just remember that the quantity of crackers each recipe produces will change, depending on the shape you choose. If the cutter is similar in size to a two-inch circle, then the number of crackers will be about the same. Have fun experimenting!

CRACKER RECIPES

The Basic Recipe

The foundation for all your cracker making ideas.

YIELD: APPROXIMATELY 26–30 2-INCH CIRCLES

BAKE: 350° FOR 15–18 MINUTES OR UNTIL GOLDEN BROWN ON BOTTOM

1¼ C. unbleached all-purpose flour
½ tsp. salt
2 T. oil
4 T. liquid
Flavorings and spices to blend into mixture or sprinkle on top
Extra all-purpose flour for rolling

1. Blend together all-purpose flour and salt.
2. Add oil and liquid.
3. Blend wet ingredients into dry ingredients until a soft dough is formed.
4. Sprinkle rolling surface with all-purpose flour and roll dough to ⅛-inch thickness.
5. Cut dough into 2-inch circles.
6. Place dough on ungreased cookie sheets.
7. Re-form dough scraps into a ball, re-roll, and cut into circles until all dough is used.
8. Prick circles two or three times with the tines of a fork.
9. Bake until golden brown on the bottom.

HELPFUL TIPS

THE MAIN THING TO REMEMBER when making crackers is to keep the ratios the same. It doesn't really matter what kind of flour, oil, or liquid you use, as long as the proportions of one to the other are about the same so that the dough that forms is soft and pliable to roll and bakes into a crisp cracker. Measuring for recipes is an approximation; if you feel the texture is too dry because you added a little bit more flour, add a few drops more liquid to soften that dry flour. If the mixture is sticky and won't form into a smooth dough, then add a sprinkle or two of flour to absorb the moisture.

If you use a little more oil, the crackers will be slightly greasier when baked. If you use more water, they'll be crunchier. Increasing the liquids will mean a slight increase in the amount of flour needed to produce a smooth dough that holds together for rolling. If you use milk instead of water, the crackers will be slightly softer and richer. I have developed all the cracker recipes in this book without milk because I'm lactose-intolerant, but you can substitute milk for the water in almost all of these recipes.

Once you've blended the dry ingredients together, you can add the wet ingredients directly to the same bowl, one by one. Just be sure to blend the resulting dough thoroughly so all the ingredients are evenly distributed.

If you want to use a low-gluten flour such as buckwheat or millet, make sure to blend in some all-purpose flour so the dough that forms is pliable enough to roll.

Mixing the ingredients by hand allows you to knead the dough for a few seconds, ensuring a smooth texture for rolling.

Feel free to sprinkle seeds and chopped nuts on top of these crackers as well as adding them into the dough. Try poppy seeds on the Whole Wheat Crackers (page XX) or sesame seeds on the Green Tea and Brown Rice Crackers (page XX). Lightly brushing each cracker with water will help the seeds to stick during the baking process.

After cutting out your first shapes, be sure to re-roll the dough scraps so that you use every bit of dough. The quantities for the recipes are based on using all the dough and a 2-inch circle cutter. If you use a smaller cutter, your yield will be greater. Likewise, if you use a much larger cutter or a different shape altogether, then your yields will be different from those listed.

The thickness of the cracker given in each recipe is an approximate measure. If your crackers are a little thicker, just remember to increase the baking times a bit. The main thing is to make sure the crackers bake long enough so that the bottoms are golden brown. If you roll the dough thicker, the recipe will yield slightly fewer crackers than what's listed in the recipes.

Like any kind of cracker, these need to be stored in an airtight container to prevent them getting soggy. I use plastic tubs and include a small scrap of paper in each with the name of the recipe on it, so that members of my family can quickly and easily find their favorite flavor.

Try some or all of the recipes I've developed and then try some of your own. Be bold and combine your favorite flavors into a crispy cracker that belongs in your recipe file.

SOME THOUGHTS ON GLUTEN-FREE CRACKERS

MANY PEOPLE ARE NOT ABLE TO EAT CRACKERS, as the gluten in the wheat causes digestive problems. I thought it would be helpful to include a Basic Gluten-Free Recipe, opposite, for those who wish to try their hand at another type of cracker. This recipe is similar to the others in this book, but by substituting white rice flour for the all-purpose flour and adding almond meal, it really is difficult to tell that this cracker has no gluten in it. Feel free to play around and exchange the Italian seasonings I used, with flavors and ideas of your very own. You can easily create a variety of gluten-free crackers by using the Basic Gluten-Free Recipe and incorporating the seasonings of many of the other cracker recipes found here.

The Basic Gluten-Free Recipe

For those looking for a crisp and flavorful gluten-free cracker, try these!

YIELD: APPROXIMATELY 24–30 2-INCH CIRCLES
BAKE: 350° FOR 15–18 MINUTES OR UNTIL GOLDEN BROWN ON BOTTOM

½ C. millet flour
½ C. white rice flour
¼ C. almond meal
Flavorings and spices to blend into mixture or sprinkle on top
¼ tsp. salt
2 T. olive oil
4 T. water
Extra white rice flour for rolling

1. Blend together millet and white rice flours, almond meal, seasonings, and salt.
2. Add olive oil and water.
3. Blend together until a soft dough is formed.
4. Sprinkle rolling surface with white rice flour and roll dough to ⅛-inch thickness.
5. Cut dough into 2-inch circles.
6. Place dough on ungreased cookie sheets.
7. Re-form dough scraps into a ball, re-roll, and cut into circles until all dough is used.
8. Prick circles two or three times with the tines of a fork.
9. Bake until golden brown on the bottom.

Almond Lover's Crackers

A slightly sweet cracker full of chopped almonds and almond milk.

YIELD: 24–28 2-INCH CIRCLES

BAKE: 350° FOR 15–20 MINUTES OR UNTIL GOLDEN BROWN ON BOTTOM

1¼ C. unbleached all-purpose flour
½ tsp. salt
½ C. finely chopped almonds (a food processor works
    well to chop almonds)
2 T. canola oil
4 T. almond milk
½ tsp. almond extract
Extra all-purpose flour for rolling

1. Mix together almonds, all-purpose flour, and salt.
2. Add canola oil, almond milk, and almond extract.
3. Blend wet ingredients into dry ingredients until a soft dough is formed.
4. Sprinkle rolling surface with all-purpose flour and roll dough to ⅛-inch thickness.
5. Cut dough into 2-inch circles.
6. Place circles on ungreased cookie sheets.
7. Re-form dough scraps into a ball, re-roll, and cut into circles until all dough is used.
8. Prick each circle two or three times with the tines of a fork.
9. Bake until golden brown on the bottom.

Bacon Crackers

Crunchy bits of bacon swirled through a cornmeal cracker are delicious served with slices of fresh tomato.

YIELD: APPROXIMATELY 24–30 2-INCH CIRCLES
BAKE: 350° FOR 15–18 MINUTES OR UNTIL GOLDEN BROWN ON BOTTOM

½ C. unbleached all-purpose flour
¾ C. cornmeal
¼ tsp. salt
½ C. cooked, crumbled bacon (bacon slices may be chopped fine with a knife)
2 T. olive oil
4 T. water
Extra all-purpose flour for rolling

1. Blend together all-purpose flour, cornmeal, and salt.
2. Add crumbled bacon bits, olive oil, and water.
3. Blend wet ingredients into dry ingredients until a soft dough is formed.
4. Sprinkle rolling surface with all-purpose flour and roll dough to ⅛-inch thickness. Bacon bits may cause dough to stick, so extra flour may be needed.
5. Cut dough into 2-inch circles.
6. Place dough on ungreased cookie sheets.
7. Re-form dough scraps into a ball, re-roll, and cut into circles until all dough is used.
8. Prick circles two or three times with the tines of a fork.
9. Bake until golden brown on the bottom.

Balsamic Vinegar and Brown Rice Crackers

Tangy and crisp-perfect with a tossed salad.

YIELD: APPROXIMATELY 28–30 2-INCH CIRCLES

BAKE: 350° FOR 15–18 MINUTES OR UNTIL GOLDEN BROWN ON BOTTOM

½ C. brown rice flour
¾ C. unbleached all-purpose flour
½ tsp. salt
2 T. olive oil
4 T. balsamic vinegar
Extra all-purpose flour for rolling

1. Mix together brown rice and all-purpose flours, and salt.
2. Add olive oil and balsamic vinegar.
3. Blend wet ingredients into dry ingredients until a soft dough is formed.
4. Sprinkle rolling surface with all-purpose flour and roll dough to ⅛- thickness.
5. Cut dough into 2-inch circles.
6. Place circles on ungreased cookie sheets.
7. Re-form dough scraps into a ball, re-roll, and cut into circles until all dough is used.
8. Prick each circle two or three times with the tines of a fork.
9. Bake until golden brown on the bottom.

Barbecue Crackers

Perfect for the barbecue lover in the house, a sweet and spicy cracker great with dips.

YIELD: APPROXIMATELY 30–36 2-INCH CIRCLES

BAKE: 350° FOR 15–18 MINUTES OR UNTIL GOLDEN BROWN ON BOTTOM

1¼ C. unbleached all-purpose flour
1 tsp. garlic salt
¼ tsp. ground black pepper
¼ tsp. chili powder
¼ tsp. ginger powder
2 tsp. prepared yellow mustard
2 T. ketchup
1 T. molasses
1 T. water
2 T. canola oil
Extra all-purpose flour for rolling

1. Mix together all-purpose flour, garlic salt, black pepper, chili powder, and ginger.
2. Add mustard, ketchup, molasses, water, and canola oil.
3. Blend wet ingredients into dry ingredients until a soft dough is formed.
4. Sprinkle rolling surface with all-purpose flour and roll dough to ⅛-inch thickness.
5. Cut dough into 2-inch circles.
6. Place circles on ungreased cookie sheets.
7. Re-form dough scraps into a ball, re-roll, and cut into circles until all dough is used.
8. Prick each circle two or three times with the tines of a fork.
9. Bake until golden brown on the bottom.

Beer and Rye Crackers

Your favorite dark beer blends with rye in this robust cracker.
Great served with wedges of Swiss cheese.

YIELD: Approximately 24–30 2-inch circles
BAKE: 350° for 15–18 minutes or until golden brown on bottom

¾ C. dark rye flour
½ C. unbleached all-purpose flour
½ tsp. salt
2 T. canola oil
4 T. dark beer
Extra all-purpose flour for rolling

1. Mix together rye and all-purpose flours, and salt.
2. Add canola oil and beer.
3. Blend wet ingredients into dry ingredients until a soft dough is formed.
4. Sprinkle rolling surface with all-purpose flour and roll dough to ⅛-inch thickness.
5. Cut dough into 2-inch circles.
6. Place circles on ungreased cookie sheets.
7. Re-form dough scraps into a ball, re-roll, and cut into circles until all dough is used.
8. Prick each circle two or three times with the tines of a fork.
9. Bake until golden brown on the bottom.

Note: For those who prefer, a light amber beer will impart a more subtle flavor.

Black Olive Crackers

Full of bits of black olive, these black speckled crackers are good with pepperoni or pieces of smoked ham.

YIELD: Approximately 30–36 2-inch crackers

BAKE: 350° for 15–18 minutes or until golden brown on bottom

1¼ C. unbleached all-purpose flour
½ tsp. onion powder
½ tsp. garlic salt
½ C. minced black olives (a food processor works well for this)
2 T. olive oil
4 T. water
Extra all-purpose flour for rolling

1. Mix together all-purpose flour, onion powder, garlic salt, and black olives.
2. Add olive oil and water.
3. Blend wet ingredients into dry ingredients until a soft dough is formed.
4. Sprinkle rolling surface with all-purpose flour and roll dough to ⅛-inch thickness.
5. Cut dough into 2-inch circles. (You may need to press harder with cutter because of olive pieces.)
6. Place circles on ungreased cookie sheets.
7. Re-form dough scraps into a ball, re-roll, and cut into circles until all dough is used.
8. Prick each circle two or three times with the tines of a fork.
9. Bake until golden brown on the bottom.

Black Pepper and Rye Crackers

For the black pepper lovers in the crowd, this recipe mixes dark rye with black pepper for a hot and spicy cracker. Try serving with your favorite cream cheese spread.

YIELD: 30–36 2-INCH CIRCLES
BAKE: 350° FOR 15–18 MINUTES OR UNTIL GOLDEN BROWN ON BOTTOM

¾ C. dark rye flour
½ C. unbleached all-purpose flour
½ tsp. salt
1 tsp. ground black pepper (cracked black pepper may be substituted)
2 T. canola oil
4 T. water
Extra all-purpose flour for rolling

1. Blend together rye flour, all-purpose flour, salt, and black pepper.
2. Add oil and water to flour mixture.
3. Blend wet ingredients into dry ingredients until a soft dough is formed.
4. Sprinkle rolling surface with all-purpose flour and roll dough to ⅛-inch thickness.
5. Cut dough into 2-inch circles.
6. Place circles on ungreased cookie sheets.
7. Re-form dough scraps into a ball, re-roll, and cut into circles until all dough is used.
8. Prick circles two or three times with the tines of a fork.
9. Bake until golden brown on the bottom.

Blue Cornmeal and Red Pepper Crackers

The distinct taste of blue corn combined with a dose of dried red pepper creates a spicy mix.

YIELD: APPROXIMATELY 28–30 2-INCH CIRCLES
BAKE: 350° FOR 15–18 MINUTES OR UNTIL GOLDEN BROWN ON BOTTOM

½ C. blue cornmeal
¾ C. unbleached all-purpose flour
½ tsp. salt
1 tsp. dried red pepper
2 T. olive oil
4 T. water
Extra all-purpose flour for rolling

1. Mix together blue cornmeal, all-purpose flour, salt, and dried red pepper.
2. Add olive oil and water.
3. Blend wet ingredients into dry ingredients until a soft dough is formed.
4. Sprinkle rolling area with all-purpose flour and roll dough to ⅛-inch thickness.
5. Cut dough into 2-inch circles.
6. Place circles on ungreased cookie sheets.
7. Re-form dough scraps into a ball, re-roll, and cut into circles until all dough is used.
8. Prick each circle two or three times with the tines of a fork.
9. Bake until golden brown on the bottom.

Caraway and Rye Crackers

The tangy taste of caraway blends with a hint of molasses in this rich rye-flavored cracker. Great served with wedges of Swiss cheese.

YIELD: APPROXIMATELY 30–36 2-INCH CIRCLES
BAKE: 350° FOR 15–18 MINUTES OR UNTIL GOLDEN BROWN ON BOTTOM

¾ C. dark rye flour
½ C. unbleached all-purpose flour
¼ tsp. salt
1 tsp. caraway seeds
1 T. molasses
2 T. canola oil
4 T. water
Extra all-purpose flour for rolling

1. Mix together rye and all-purpose flours, salt, and caraway seeds.
2. Add molasses, canola oil, and water.
3. Blend wet ingredients into dry ingredients until a soft dough is formed.
4. Sprinkle rolling area with all-purpose flour and roll dough to ⅛-inch thickness.
5. Cut dough into 2-inch circles.
6. Place circles on ungreased cookie sheets.
7. Re-form dough scraps into a ball, re-roll, and cut into circles until all dough is used.
8. Prick each circle two or three times with the tines of a fork.
9. Bake until golden brown on the bottom.

Note: For those who like even more caraway flavor, lightly brush the top of each cracker with water, then sprinkle additional seeds on top before baking.

Cardamom and Whole Wheat Crackers

The almost peppery taste of cardamom blends well with whole wheat for an Old World–flavored cracker.

YIELD: APPROXIMATELY 28–30 2-INCH CIRCLES
BAKE: 350° FOR 15–18 MINUTES OR UNTIL GOLDEN BROWN ON BOTTOM

½ C. whole wheat flour
¾ C. unbleached all-purpose flour
½ tsp. salt
1 tsp. cardamom
2 T. canola oil
4 T. water
Extra all-purpose flour for rolling

1. Mix together whole wheat and all-purpose flours, salt, and cardamom.
2. Add canola oil and water.
3. Blend wet ingredients into dry ingredients until a soft dough is formed.
4. Sprinkle rolling area with all-purpose flour and roll dough to ⅛-inch thickness.
5. Cut dough into 2-inch circles.
6. Place circles on ungreased cookie sheets.
7. Re-form dough scraps into a ball, re-roll, and cut into circles until all dough is used.
8. Prick each circle two or three times with the tines of a fork.
9. Bake until golden brown on the bottom.

Carrot and Ginger Crackers

An orange-yellow cracker with the bite of spicy ginger.

YIELD: 36 2-INCH CIRCLES

BAKE: 350° FOR 15–18 MINUTES OR UNTIL GOLDEN BROWN ON BOTTOM

1¼ C. unbleached all-purpose flour
½ tsp. salt
2 tsp. powdered ginger
2 T. canola oil
3½–4 T. pure carrot juice (available by the bottle in
   the produce section)
Extra all-purpose flour for rolling

1. Mix together all-purpose flour, salt, and powdered ginger.
2. Add canola oil and carrot juice.
3. Blend wet ingredients into dry ingredients until a soft dough is formed.
4. Sprinkle rolling surface with all-purpose flour and roll dough to
   ⅛-inch thickness.
5. Cut dough into 2-inch circles.
6. Place circles on ungreased cookie sheets.
7. Re-form dough scraps into a ball, re-roll, and cut into circles until all
   dough is used.
8. Prick each circle two or three times with the tines of a fork.
9. Bake until golden brown on the bottom.

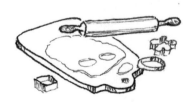

Carrot and Millet Crackers

A mild cracker rich in color and the sweet flavor of millet and carrot.

YIELD: Approximately 30–36 2-inch circles

BAKE: 350° for 15–18 minutes or until golden brown on bottom

¾ C. millet flour
¾ C. unbleached all-purpose flour
1 tsp. powdered ginger
½ tsp. salt
2 T. olive oil
4 T. pure carrot juice (available by the bottle in the produce section)
Extra all-purpose flour for rolling

1. Blend together millet flour, all-purpose flour, ginger, and salt.
2. Add olive oil and carrot juice.
3. Blend wet ingredients into dry ingredients until a soft dough is formed. If mixture is still too sticky, add a little more all-purpose flour.
4. Sprinkle rolling surface with all-purpose flour and roll dough to ⅛-inch thickness.
5. Cut into 2-inch circles.
6. Place circles on ungreased cookie sheets.
7. Re-form dough scraps into a ball, re-roll, and cut into circles until all dough is used.
8. Prick each circle two or three times with the tines of a fork.
9. Bake until golden brown.

Cheddar Cheese Crackers

Tangy extra-sharp cheddar cheese with just a hint of spicy yellow mustard.

YIELD: APPROXIMATELY 30–40 2-INCH CIRCLES

BAKE: 350° FOR 15–18 MINUTES OR UNTIL GOLDEN BROWN ON BOTTOM

1¼ C. unbleached all-purpose flour

½ tsp. salt

½ C. finely grated extra-sharp cheddar cheese
(preferably Cabot brand, which is lactose-free)

2 T. olive oil

2–3 tsp. prepared yellow mustard

5 T. water

Extra all-purpose flour for rolling

1. Mix all-purpose flour, salt, and cheddar cheese.
2. Add olive oil, mustard, and water.
3. Blend wet ingredients into dry ingredients until a soft dough is formed.
4. Sprinkle rolling surface with all-purpose flour and roll dough to ⅛-inch thickness.
5. Cut dough into 2-inch circles.
6. Place circles on ungreased cookie sheets.
7. Re-form dough scraps into a ball, re-roll, and cut into circles until all dough is used.
8. Prick each circle two or three times with the tines of a fork.
9. Bake until golden brown on the bottom.

Note: For those who are not lactose-intolerant, other brands of cheese can be substituted for the Cabot. Also, other types of cheese can be used in place of the cheddar for a new variety of cheese cracker.

Chicken Bouillon Crackers

The rich taste of chicken soup in a crunchy cracker. Try these topped with a slice of avocado.

YIELD: Approximately 30–36 2-inch crackers
BAKE: 350° for 12–15 minutes or until golden brown on bottom

4 chicken bouillon cubes
¼ C. boiling water
1¼ C. unbleached all-purpose flour
2 T. canola oil
Extra all-purpose flour for rolling

1. Dissolve chicken bouillon cubes in boiling water in bottom of mixing bowl.
2. When thoroughly dissolved, stir in flour and canola oil.
3. Blend wet ingredients into dry ingredients until a soft dough is formed.
4. Sprinkle rolling surface with all-purpose flour and roll dough to ⅛-inch thickness.
5. Cut dough into 2-inch circles.
6. Place circles on ungreased cookie sheets.
7. Re-form dough scraps into a ball, re-roll, and cut into circles until all dough is used.
8. Prick each circle two to three times with the tines of a fork.
9. Bake until golden on the bottom.

Cocoa and Whole Wheat Crackers

Chocolaty, nutty, crunchy . . . yum.

YIELD: APPROXIMATELY 28–30 2-INCH CIRCLES
BAKE: 350° FOR 15–18 MINUTES OR UNTIL GOLDEN BROWN ON BOTTOM

¼ C. cocoa flour
⅓ C. whole wheat flour
½ C. unbleached all-purpose flour
½ tsp. salt
2 T. granulated sugar
½ tsp. cinnamon
2 T. canola oil
4 T. water
Extra all-purpose flour for rolling

1. Mix together cocoa, whole wheat, and all-purpose flours, salt, sugar, and cinnamon.
2. Add canola oil and water.
3. Blend wet ingredients into dry ingredients until a soft dough is formed.
4. Sprinkle rolling area with all-purpose flour and roll dough to ⅛-inch thickness.
5. Cut dough into 2-inch circles.
6. Place circles on ungreased cookie sheets.
7. Re-form dough scraps into a ball, re-roll, and cut into circles until all dough is used.
8. Prick each circle two or three times with the tines of a fork.
9. Bake until golden brown on the bottom.

Coffee and Dark Rye Crackers

Somewhat bitter, rich, and robust coffee combined with hearty rye creates an unusual combination.

YIELD: APPROXIMATELY 28–30 2-INCH CIRCLES
BAKE: 350° FOR 15–18 MINUTES OR UNTIL GOLDEN BROWN ON BOTTOM

½ C. dark rye flour
¾ C. unbleached all-purpose flour
½ tsp. salt
2–3 T. instant coffee dissolved in 5 T. water or 4–5 T. cooled coffee
2 T. olive oil
Extra all-purpose flour for rolling

1. Mix together dark rye and all-purpose flours, and salt.
2. Add coffee and olive oil.
3. Blend wet ingredients into dry ingredients until a soft dough is formed.
4. Sprinkle rolling area with all-purpose flour and roll dough to ⅛-inch thickness.
5. Cut dough into 2-inch circles.
6. Place circles on ungreased cookie sheets.
7. Re-form dough scraps into a ball, re-roll, and cut into circles until all dough is used.
8. Prick each circle two or three times with the tines of a fork.
9. Bake until golden brown on the bottom.

Curry and Brown Rice Crackers

Not for the faint of heart . . . Spicy curry blends with the rich taste of brown rice creating a brilliant yellow, hot in-the-back-of-the-throat cracker. Great served with hummus.

YIELD: APPROXIMATELY 30–36 2-INCH CIRCLES

BAKE: 350° FOR 15–18 MINUTES OR UNTIL GOLDEN BROWN ON BOTTOM

¾ C. unbleached all-purpose flour

½ C. brown rice flour

1½ tsp. curry powder (for those wishing a milder cracker, use ¾–1 tsp. curry)

½ tsp. salt

2 T. olive oil

4 T. water

Extra all-purpose flour for rolling

1. Blend together all-purpose flour, brown rice flour, curry powder, and salt.
2. Add olive oil and water to dry ingredients.
3. Blend wet ingredients into dry ingredients until a soft dough is formed.
4. Sprinkle all-purpose flour on rolling surface and roll dough to ⅛-inch thickness.
5. Cut dough into 2-inch circles.
6. Place circles on ungreased cookie sheets.
7. Re-form dough scraps into a ball, re-roll, and cut into circles until all dough is used.
8. Prick circles two or three times with the tines of a fork.
9. Bake until golden brown.

Dried Cranberry and Graham Crackers

Small flecks of tart cranberry swirled in a graham flour base.

YIELD: Approximately 28–30 2-inch circles
BAKE: 350° for 18–22 minutes or until golden brown on bottom

½ C. graham flour
¾ C. unbleached all-purpose flour
½ tsp. salt
½ tsp. cinnamon
¼ C. dried cranberries, finely chopped
2 T. canola oil
4 T. water
Extra all-purpose flour for rolling

1. Mix together graham and all-purpose flours, salt, and cinnamon.
2. Add chopped cranberries, canola oil, and water.
3. Blend wet ingredients into dry ingredients until a soft dough is formed.
4. Sprinkle rolling area with all-purpose flour and roll dough to ⅛-inch thickness.
5. Cut dough into 2-inch circles.
6. Place circles on ungreased cookie sheets.
7. Re-form dough scraps into a ball, re-roll, and cut into circles until all dough is used.
8. Prick each circle two or three times with the tines of a fork.
9. Bake until golden brown on the bottom.

Note: This dough is a bit stiff and requires a little extra effort to roll into a thin layer for cutting. The end result may be a bit thicker than other crackers and will need more baking time.

Graham Crackers

Sprinkled with granulated sugar, these crackers are great dipped in tea or coffee or used for a batch of homemade s'mores.

YIELD: 30–36 2-INCH CIRCLES
BAKE: 350° FOR 15–18 MINUTES OR UNTIL GOLDEN BROWN ON BOTTOM

¾ C. graham flour
½ C. unbleached all-purpose flour
1½ tsp. cinnamon
2 T. blackstrap molasses
2 T. canola oil
3 T. water
Extra all-purpose flour for rolling
Granulated sugar to sprinkle on top

1. Mix together graham flour, all-purpose flour, and cinnamon.
2. Add molasses, canola oil, and water to dry ingredients.
3. Blend wet ingredients into dry ingredients until a soft dough is formed.
4. Sprinkle rolling surface with all-purpose flour and roll dough to ⅛-inch thickness.
5. Cut dough into 2-inch circles.
6. Place circles on ungreased cookie sheets.
7. Re-form dough scraps into a ball, re-roll, and cut into circles until all dough is used.
8. Prick each circle two or three times with the tines of a fork.
9. Sprinkle granulated sugar on top of each cracker.
10. Bake until golden brown on the bottom.

Green Tea and Brown Rice Crackers

The subtle taste of green tea blends nicely with the mild flavor of brown rice in these crispy crackers.

YIELD: 30–36 2-INCH CIRCLES

BAKE: 350° FOR 15–18 MINUTES OR UNTIL GOLDEN BROWN ON BOTTOM

½ C. brown rice flour

¾ C. unbleached all-purpose flour

½ tsp. salt

6 green tea bags (remove tea from bags and place tea in mixing bowl) or about 2 T. green tea

2 T. canola oil

4 T. water

Extra all-purpose flour for rolling

1. Mix together dry green tea, brown rice flour, all-purpose flour, and salt.
2. Add canola oil and water.
3. Blend wet ingredients into dry ingredients until a soft dough is formed.
4. Sprinkle rolling surface with all-purpose flour and roll dough to ⅛-inch thickness.
5. Cut dough into 2-inch circles.
6. Place circles on ungreased cookie sheets.
7. Re-form dough scraps into a ball, re-roll, and cut into circles until all dough is used.
8. Prick each circle two or three times with the tines of a fork.
9. Bake until golden brown on the bottom.

Guacamole Crackers

The flavors of chili, cumin, and garlic blend together in this cracker, which tastes great with a slice of fresh avocado on top.

YIELD: 30–36 2-INCH CIRCLES

BAKE: 350° FOR 15–18 MINUTES OR UNTIL GOLDEN BROWN ON BOTTOM

½ C. cornmeal
¾ C. unbleached all-purpose flour
¾ tsp. garlic salt
1½ tsp. cumin
¼ tsp. chili powder
2 T. canola oil
2 T. lemon juice
2 T. water

1. Mix together cornmeal, all-purpose flour, garlic salt, cumin, and chili powder.
2. Add canola oil, lemon juice, and water.
3. Blend wet ingredients into dry ingredients until a soft dough is formed.
4. Sprinkle rolling surface with all-purpose flour and roll dough to ⅛-inch thickness.
5. Cut dough into 2-inch circles.
6. Place circles on ungreased cookie sheets.
7. Re-form dough scraps into a ball, re-roll, and cut into circles until all dough is used.
8. Prick each circle two or three times with the tines of a fork.
9. Bake until golden brown on the bottom.

Honey and Thyme Crackers

A touch of honey, the taste of thyme, and the healthy goodness of graham flour.

YIELD: APPROXIMATELY 28–30 2-INCH CIRCLES
BAKE: 350° FOR 15–18 MINUTES OR UNTIL GOLDEN BROWN ON BOTTOM

½ C. graham flour
¾ C. unbleached all-purpose flour
½ tsp. salt
2 tsp. dried thyme
1 T. honey
2 T. canola oil
4 T. water
Extra all-purpose flour for rolling

1. Mix together graham and all-purpose flours, salt, and thyme.
2. Add honey, canola oil, and water.
3. Blend wet ingredients into dry ingredients until a soft dough is formed.
4. Sprinkle rolling area with all-purpose flour and roll dough to ⅛-inch thickness.
5. Cut dough into 2-inch circles.
6. Place circles on ungreased cookie sheets.
7. Re-form dough scraps into a ball, re-roll, and cut into circles until all dough is used.
8. Prick each circle two or three times with the tines of a fork.
9. Bake until golden brown on the bottom.

Hungarian Paprika and Cornmeal Crackers

Reddish in color, this is a spicy cracker!

YIELD: APPROXIMATELY 28–30 2-INCH CIRCLES
BAKE: 350° FOR 15–18 MINUTES OR UNTIL GOLDEN BROWN ON BOTTOM

½ C. cornmeal
¾ C. unbleached all-purpose flour
2–3 tsp. Hungarian paprika
½ tsp. salt
2 T. olive oil
4 T. water
Extra all-purpose flour for rolling

1. Mix together cornmeal, all-purpose flour, Hungarian paprika, and salt.
2. Add olive oil and water.
3. Blend wet ingredients into dry ingredients until a soft dough is formed.
4. Sprinkle rolling area with all-purpose flour and roll dough to ⅛-inch thickness.
5. Cut dough into 2-inch circles.
6. Place circles on ungreased cookie sheets.
7. Re-form dough scraps into a ball, re-roll, and cut into circles until all dough is used.
8. Prick each circle two or three times with the tines of a fork.
9. Bake until golden brown on the bottom.

Kelp and Brown Rice Crackers

A sea-salty cracker reminiscent of days on the beach.

YIELD: APPROXIMATELY 28–30 2-INCH CIRCLES
BAKE: 350° FOR 15–18 MINUTES OR UNTIL GOLDEN BROWN ON BOTTOM

½ C. brown rice flour
¾ C. unbleached all-purpose flour
2 tsp. kelp powder
½ tsp. salt
2 T. canola oil
4 T. water
Extra all-purpose flour for rolling

1. Mix together brown rice and all-purpose flours, kelp, and salt.
2. Add canola oil and water.
3. Blend wet ingredients into dry ingredients until a soft dough is formed.
4. Sprinkle rolling area with all-purpose flour and roll dough to ⅛-inch thickness.
5. Cut dough into 2-inch circles.
6. Place circles on ungreased cookie sheets.
7. Re-form dough scraps into a ball, re-roll, and cut into circles until all dough is used.
8. Prick each circle two or three times with the tines of a fork.
9. Bake until golden brown on the bottom.

Lemon Crackers

I love lemon meringue pie, and these crackers have that same sweet-tart lemony flavor.

YIELD: Approximately 28–30 2-inch circles
BAKE: 350° for 15–18 minutes or until golden brown on bottom

1¼ C. unbleached all-purpose flour
½ tsp. salt
2 T. sugar
2 T. canola oil
4 T. lemon juice
2–3 drops pure lemon oil
Extra all-purpose flour for rolling

1. Mix together all-purpose flour, salt, and sugar.
2. Add canola oil, lemon juice, and lemon oil.
3. Blend wet ingredients into dry ingredients until a soft dough is formed.
4. Sprinkle rolling area with all-purpose flour and roll dough to ⅛-inch thickness.
5. Cut dough into 2-inch circles.
6. Place circles on ungreased cookie sheets.
7. Re-form dough scraps into a ball, re-roll, and cut into circles until all dough is used.
8. Prick each circle two or three times with the tines of a fork.
9. Bake until golden brown on the bottom.

Lemon and Dill Crackers

The zippy taste of lemon blends with dill, making this cracker the perfect companion for a piece of smoked salmon.

YIELD: APPROXIMATELY 30–36 2-INCH CIRCLES

BAKE: 350° FOR 15–18 MINUTES OR UNTIL GOLDEN BROWN ON BOTTOM

1¼ C. unbleached all-purpose flour
½ tsp. salt
2 tsp. dried dill weed
2 T. canola oil
3 T. lemon juice
2 T. water
Extra all-purpose flour for rolling

1. Mix together all-purpose flour, salt, and dill.
2. Add oil, lemon juice, and water.
3. Blend wet ingredients into dry ingredients until a soft dough is formed.
4. Sprinkle unbleached flour on rolling surface and roll dough to ⅛-inch thickness.
5. Cut dough into 2-inch circles.
6. Place circles on ungreased cookie sheets.
7. Re-form dough scraps into a ball, re-roll, and cut into circles until all dough is used.
8. Prick each circle two or three times with the tines of a fork.
9. Bake until golden brown on the bottom.

Lemon and Poppy Seed Crackers

These tangy crackers full of rich poppy seeds and the nutty taste of whole wheat are great with a bit of smoked shrimp.

YIELD: 30–36 2-INCH CIRCLES
BAKE: 350° FOR 15–18 MINUTES OR UNTIL GOLDEN BROWN ON BOTTOM

½ C. whole wheat flour
¾ C. unbleached all-purpose flour
2 T. poppy seeds
½ tsp. salt
3 T. lemon juice
2 T. water
2 T. olive oil
Extra all-purpose flour for rolling

1. Mix together whole wheat flour, all-purpose flour, poppy seeds, and salt.
2. Add lemon juice, water, and olive oil.
3. Blend wet ingredients into dry ingredients until a soft dough is formed.
4. Sprinkle rolling surface with all-purpose flour and roll dough to ⅛-inch thickness.
5. Cut dough into 2-inch circles.
6. Place circles on ungreased cookie sheets.
7. Re-form dough scraps into a ball ball, re-roll, and cut into circles until all dough is used.
8. Prick each circle two or three times with the tines of a fork.
9. Bake until golden brown on the bottom.

Maple and Sage Crackers

Hints of maple syrup and sage are reminiscent of stuffing in this slightly sweet cracker.

YIELD: APPROXIMATELY 28–30 2-INCH CIRCLES
BAKE: 350° FOR 15–18 MINUTES OR UNTIL GOLDEN BROWN ON BOTTOM

½ C. barley flour
¾ C. unbleached all-purpose flour
½ tsp. salt
1 tsp. dried powdered sage
2 T. canola oil
3 T. maple syrup
1 T. water
Extra all-purpose flour for rolling

1. Mix together barley and all-purpose flours, salt, and sage.
2. Add canola oil, maple syrup, and water.
3. Blend wet ingredients into dry ingredients until a soft dough is formed.
4. Sprinkle rolling area with all-purpose flour and roll dough to ⅛-inch thickness.
5. Cut dough into 2-inch circles.
6. Place circles on ungreased cookie sheets.
7. Re-form dough scraps into a ball, re-roll, and cut into circles until all dough is used.
8. Prick each circle two or three times with the tines of a fork.
9. Bake until golden brown on the bottom.

Maple and Walnut Crackers

Walnuts and maple syrup—perfect with an after-dinner dessert wine and cheese.

YIELD: Approximately 28–30 2-inch circles
BAKE: 350° for 15–18 minutes or until golden brown on bottom

1¼ C. unbleached all-purpose flour
½ tsp. salt
½ C. finely ground walnuts
2 T. canola oil
3 T. maple syrup
2 T. water
Extra all-purpose flour for rolling

1. Mix together walnuts, all-purpose flour, and salt.
2. Add canola oil, maple syrup, and water.
3. Blend wet ingredients into dry ingredients until a soft dough is formed.
4. Sprinkle rolling area with all-purpose flour and roll dough to ⅛-inch thickness.
5. Cut dough into 2-inch circles.
6. Place circles on ungreased cookie sheets.
7. Re-form dough scraps into a ball, re-roll, and cut into circles until all dough is used.
8. Prick each circle two or three times with the tines of a fork.
9. Bake until golden brown on the bottom.

Mint Crackers

Peppermint in a cracker? Yes . . . delicious on its own or served with cream cheese, these are also good for a sick stomach.

YIELD: APPROXIMATELY 26–30 2-INCH CIRCLES

BAKE: 350° FOR 15–18 MINUTES OR UNTIL GOLDEN BROWN ON BOTTOM

1¼ C. unbleached all-purpose flour

½ tsp. salt

6 peppermint tea bags, opened, or 2 T. dried peppermint, finely ground

2 T. canola oil

4–5 T. water (the tea absorbs some of the liquid, so a little more water might be needed)

Extra all-purpose flour for rolling

1. Mix together peppermint, all-purpose flour, and salt.
2. Add canola oil and water.
3. Blend wet ingredients into dry ingredients until a soft dough is formed.
4. Sprinkle rolling area with all-purpose flour and roll dough to ⅛-inch thickness.
5. Cut dough into 2-inch circles.
6. Place circles on ungreased cookie sheets.
7. Re-form dough scraps into a ball, re-roll, and cut into circles until all dough is used.
8. Prick each circle two or three times with the tines of a fork.
9. Bake until golden brown on the bottom.

Mole Crackers

Mole is a Mexican blend of hot peppers, oil, spices, and chocolate. This cracker combines mole with cornmeal for a spicy, bite-in-the-back-of-the-throat Mexican treat.

YIELD: APPROXIMATELY 30–36 2-INCH CRACKERS
BAKE: 350° FOR 15–18 MINUTES OR UNTIL GOLDEN BROWN ON BOTTOM

¾ C. unbleached all-purpose flour
½ C. cornmeal
½ tsp. salt
2 T. mole sauce
I T. canola oil
4 T. water
Extra flour for rolling

1. Mix together all-purpose flour, cornmeal, and salt.
2. Add mole and rub into flour until pea-sized pieces are formed.
3. Add canola oil and water to dry ingredients.
4. Blend wet ingredients into dry ingredients until a soft dough is formed.
5. Sprinkle rolling surface with all-purpose flour and roll to ⅛-inch thickness.
6. Cut dough into 2-inch circles.
7. Place circles on ungreased cookie sheets.
8. Re-form dough scraps into a ball, re-roll, and cut into circles until all dough is used.
9. Prick each circle two or three times with the tines of a fork.
10. Bake until golden brown on the bottom.

Multi-Grain Crackers

A rich and hearty cracker full of a variety of healthy grains.

YIELD: APPROXIMATELY 30–36 2-INCH CRACKERS

BAKE: 350° FOR 15–18 MINUTES OR UNTIL GOLDEN BROWN ON BOTTOM

½ C. whole wheat flour
¼ C. dark rye flour
¼ C. cornmeal
¼ C. unbleached all-purpose flour
½ tsp. salt
2 T. olive oil
4 T. water
Extra all-purpose flour for rolling

1. Mix together whole wheat flour, rye flour, cornmeal, all-purpose flour, and salt.
2. Add olive oil and water to flours.
3. Blend wet ingredients into dry ingredients until a dense dough is formed. This may require a little kneading by hand to form a smooth dough.
4. Sprinkle rolling surface with all-purpose flour and roll dough to ⅛-inch thickness. Dough is dense, so extra pressure may be needed to roll to proper thickness.
6. Cut dough into 2-inch circles.
7. Place circles on ungreased cookie sheets.
8. Re-form dough scraps into a ball, re-roll, and cut into circles until all dough is used.
9. Prick each circle two or three times with the tines of a fork.
10. Bake until golden brown on the bottom.

Oatmeal Crackers

Hearty oatmeal crackers similar to flat breads found in Scotland, these are a simple way to work more oats into your diet without having to eat oatmeal for breakfast.

YIELD: APPROXIMATELY 20–24 2-INCH CIRCLES
BAKE: 350° FOR 18–20 MINUTES OR UNTIL GOLDEN BROWN ON BOTTOM

¾ C. unbleached all-purpose flour
½ C. rolled oats
½ tsp. salt
1 tsp. white sugar
2 T. canola oil
3 T. hot water
Extra all-purpose flour for rolling

1. Mix together all-purpose flour, oats, salt, and sugar.
2. Add canola oil and hot water.
3. Blend wet ingredients into dry ingredients until a soft, slightly sticky dough is formed.
4. Sprinkle rolling surface generously with all-purpose flour and roll dough to ⅛-inch thickness.
5. Cut dough into 2-inch circles.
6. Place circles on ungreased cookie sheets.
7. Re-form dough scraps into a ball, re-roll, and cut into circles until all dough is used.
8. Prick each circle two or three times with the tines of a fork.
9. Bake until golden brown on the bottom.

Onion Lover's Crackers

Caramelized onion bits swirl through a rich cornmeal cracker.

YIELD: Approximately 30–36 2-inch circles
BAKE: 350° for 15–18 minutes or until golden brown on bottom

½ C. minced onion
2 T. olive oil
½ C. cornmeal
¾ C. unbleached all-purpose flour
¼ tsp. salt
½ tsp. onion powder
4 T. water
Extra all-purpose flour for rolling

1. Cook minced onion in olive oil until golden in color. Allow to cool.
2. In mixing bowl, blend together cornmeal, flour, salt, and onion powder.
3. Add cool cooked-onion-and-oil mixture to flour blend.
4. Stir in water and blend until dough is formed.
5. Sprinkle flour on rolling surface and roll dough to ⅛-inch thickness. Onion bits may cause dough to stick, so extra flour may be needed.
6. Cut dough into 2-inch circles.
7. Place circles on ungreased cookie sheets.
8. Re-form dough scraps into a ball, re-roll, and cut into circles until all dough is used.
9. Prick circles two or three times with the tines of a fork.
10. Bake until golden brown on the bottom.

Orange and Buckwheat Crackers

The sweet taste of orange blends with the strong flavor of buckwheat in these crackers reminiscent of the buckwheat pancakes I used to eat as a child.

YIELD: APPROXIMATELY 30–36 2-INCH CIRCLES

BAKE: 350° FOR 15–18 MINUTES OR UNTIL GOLDEN BROWN ON BOTTOM

½ C. unbleached all-purpose flour
¾ C. buckwheat flour
½ tsp. salt
2 T. canola oil
2 tsp. orange extract
4 T. water
Extra all-purpose flour for rolling

1. Mix together all-purpose flour, buckwheat, and salt.
2. Add canola oil, orange extract, and water.
3. Blend wet ingredients into dry ingredients until a soft dough is formed.
4. Sprinkle rolling surface with all-purpose flour and roll dough to ⅛-inch thickness.
5. Cut dough into 2-inch circles.
6. Place circles on ungreased cookie sheets.
7. Re-form dough scraps into a ball, re-roll, and cut into circles until all dough is used.
8. Prick each circle two or three times with the tines of a fork.
9. Bake until golden brown on the bottom.

Peanut Butter and Jelly Crackers

A treat for children and grown-ups alike, these are reminiscent of the jelly thumbprint cookies one sees in the stores at Christmastime.

YIELD: APPROXIMATELY 30–36 2-INCH ROUNDS
BAKE: 350° FOR 15–18 MINUTES OR UNTIL GOLDEN BROWN ON BOTTOM

1½ C. unbleached all-purpose flour
½ tsp. salt
2 T. canola oil
4 T. peanut butter
5 T. water
9 T. (more or less) favorite jam or jelly
Extra all-purpose flour for rolling

1. Mix together flour and salt.
2. Add oil, peanut butter, and water to dry ingredients.
3. Blend wet ingredients into dry ingredients until a soft dough is formed.
4. Sprinkle rolling surface with all-purpose flour and roll dough to ⅛-inch thickness.
5. Cut dough into 2-inch circles.
6. Place circles on ungreased cookie sheets.
7. Re-form dough scraps into a ball, re-roll, and cut into circles until all dough is used.
8. Top each circle with about ¼ tsp. jam or jelly.
9. Bake until golden brown on the bottom.

Pecan and Whole Wheat Crackers

A lovely speckled-brown cracker full of hearty nuts.

YIELD: APPROXIMATELY 28–30 2-INCH CIRCLES
BAKE: 350° FOR 15–18 MINUTES OR UNTIL GOLDEN BROWN ON BOTTOM

⅓ C. whole wheat flour
½ C. unbleached all-purpose flour
½ tsp. salt
½ C. finely ground pecans
2 T. canola oil
4 T. water
Extra all-purpose flour for rolling

1. Mix together pecans, whole wheat and all-purpose flours, and salt.
2. Add canola oil and water.
3. Blend wet ingredients into dry ingredients until a soft dough is formed.
4. Sprinkle rolling area with all-purpose flour and roll dough to ⅛-inch thickness.
5. Cut dough into 2-inch circles.
6. Place circles on ungreased cookie sheets.
7. Re-form dough scraps into a ball, re-roll, and cut into circles until all dough is used.
8. Prick each circle two or three times with the tines of a fork.
9. Bake until golden brown on the bottom.

Pecan Lover's Crackers

Nutty and rich, with a smooth, buttery texture, these speckled-brown crackers are sure to please the nut lover in the family.

YIELD: APPROXIMATELY 30–36 2-INCH CIRCLES
BAKE: 350° FOR 15–18 MINUTES OR UNTIL GOLDEN BROWN ON BOTTOM

¾ C. unbleached all-purpose flour
¾ C. pecan meal (available at health food stores, or grind your own from fresh pecans)
½ tsp. salt
2 T. canola oil
3 T. water
Extra all-purpose flour for rolling

1. Mix together all-purpose flour, pecan meal, and salt.
2. Add canola oil and water and blend until dough is smooth.
3. Sprinkle rolling surface with all-purpose flour and roll to ⅛-inch thickness.
4. Cut dough into 2-inch circles.
5. Place circles on ungreased cookie sheets.
6. Re-form dough scraps into a ball, re-roll, and cut into circles until all dough is used.
7. Prick each circle two or three times with the tines of a fork.
8. Bake until golden brown on the bottom.

Pistachio Crackers

For the true nut lover, as it takes a little time to shell all the pistachios.

YIELD: APPROXIMATELY 28–30 2-INCH CIRCLES
BAKE: 350° FOR 15–18 MINUTES OR UNTIL GOLDEN BROWN ON BOTTOM

1¼ C. unbleached all-purpose flour
½ tsp. salt
¼ C. finely ground pistachios
2 T. canola oil
½ tsp. almond extract
3 T. water
Extra all-purpose flour for rolling

1. Mix together pistachios, all-purpose flour, and salt.
2. Add canola oil, almond extract, and water.
3. Blend wet ingredients into dry ingredients until a soft dough is formed.
4. Sprinkle rolling area with all-purpose flour and roll dough to ⅛-inch thickness.
5. Cut dough into 2-inch circles.
6. Place circles on ungreased cookie sheets.
7. Re-form dough scraps into a ball, re-roll, and cut into circles until all dough is used.
8. Prick each circle two or three times with the tines of a fork.
9. Bake until golden brown on the bottom.

Potato and Rye Crackers

A hearty dark cracker reminiscent of a Finnish flat bread.

YIELD: APPROXIMATELY 30–36 2-INCH CIRCLES

BAKE: 350° FOR 25–35 MINUTES OR UNTIL GOLDEN BROWN ON BOTTOM

½ C. dark rye flour
¾ C. unbleached all-purpose flour
½ tsp. salt
1/3 tsp. nutmeg
½ C. mashed potatoes
2 T. canola oil
3 T. water
Extra all-purpose flour for rolling

1. Mix together rye flour, all-purpose flour, salt, and nutmeg.
2. Add mashed potatoes, canola oil, and water to dry ingredients.
3. Blend wet ingredients into dry ingredients until a soft dough is formed.
4. Sprinkle rolling surface with all-purpose flour and roll dough to ⅛-inch thickness. Depending on moisture content of potatoes, more flour may be needed; dough can be sticky.
5. Cut dough into 2-inch circles.
6. Place circles on ungreased cookie sheets.
7. Re-form dough scraps into a ball, re-roll, and cut into circles until all dough is used.
8. Prick circles two to three times with the tines of a fork.
9. Bake until golden brown on the bottom.

Note: Baking time will vary depending on the moistness of the mashed potato used in this recipe. Moist potatoes will increase the baking time; drier potatoes will reduce it.

Rosemary Crackers

The taste of rosemary brings to mind slowly baked pot roasts served with mashed potatoes.

YIELD: APPROXIMATELY 30–36 2-INCH CIRCLES
BAKE: 350° FOR 15–18 MINUTES OR UNTIL GOLDEN BROWN ON BOTTOM

1¼ C. unbleached all-purpose flour
1 tsp. dried rosemary, crumbled
½ tsp. salt
2 T. olive oil
4 T. water
Extra all-purpose flour for rolling

1. Mix together all-purpose flour, rosemary, and salt.
2. Add olive oil and water.
3. Blend wet ingredients into dry ingredients until a soft dough is formed.
4. Sprinkle all-purpose flour on surface and roll dough to ⅛-inch thickness.
5. Cut dough into 2-inch circles.
6. Place circles on ungreased cookie sheets.
7. Re-form dough scraps into a ball, re-roll, and cut into circles until all dough is used.
8. Prick circles two or three times with the tines of a fork.
9. Bake until golden brown on the bottom.

Rosewater Crackers

The delicate taste of rose in a slightly sweet cracker.

YIELD: APPROXIMATELY 28–30 2-INCH CIRCLES
BAKE: 350° FOR 15–18 MINUTES OR UNTIL GOLDEN BROWN ON BOTTOM

1¼ C. unbleached all-purpose flour
2 T. granulated sugar, plus more to sprinkle on top
½ tsp. salt
2 T. canola oil
3 T. rosewater (found in gourmet food shops)
2 T. water
Extra all-purpose flour for rolling

1. Mix together all-purpose flour, granulated sugar, and salt.
2. Add canola oil, rosewater, and water.
3. Blend wet ingredients into dry ingredients until a soft dough is formed.
4. Sprinkle rolling area with all-purpose flour and roll dough to ⅛-inch thickness.
5. Cut dough into 2-inch circles.
6. Place circles on ungreased cookie sheets.
7. Re-form dough scraps into a ball, re-roll, and cut into circles until all dough is used.
8. Prick each circle two or three times with the tines of a fork.
9. Sprinkle tops of crackers with granulated sugar.
10. Bake until golden brown on the bottom.

Salsa and Cornmeal Crackers

A spicy takeoff on the traditional fried tortilla chip dipped in salsa.
This cracker tastes great with a slice of cheddar cheese on top.

YIELD: APPROXIMATELY 30–36 2-INCH CIRCLES
BAKE: 350° FOR 15–18 MINUTES OR UNTIL GOLDEN BROWN ON BOTTOM

¾ C. unbleached all-purpose flour
½ C. cornmeal
½ tsp. salt
2 T. canola oil
3 T. hot salsa (puree with a food processor for a smoother texture
    to the cracker)
3 T. water
Extra all-purpose flour for rolling

1. Mix together all-purpose flour, cornmeal, and salt.
2. Add canola oil, salsa, and water.
3. Blend wet ingredients into dry ingredients until a soft dough is formed.
4. Sprinkle rolling area with all-purpose flour and roll dough to ⅛-inch thickness.
5. Cut dough into 2-inch circles.
6. Place circles on ungreased cookie sheets.
7. Re-form dough scraps into a ball, re-roll, and cut into circles until all dough is used.
8. Prick each circle two or three times with a fork.
9. Bake until golden brown on the bottom.

Note: For those who like things extra-spicy, a few drops of hot sauce may be added to the flour mixture at the same time as the oil.

Sesame Seed and Brown Rice Crackers

My friend Angela loves the taste of sesame. The rich flavor of sesame oil and sesame seeds blended with the buttery taste of brown rice won her approval.

YIELD: APPROXIMATELY 30–36 2-INCH CIRCLES
BAKE: 350° FOR 15–18 MINUTES OR UNTIL GOLDEN BROWN ON BOTTOM

½ C. unbleached all-purpose flour
¾ C. brown rice flour
½ tsp. salt
1½–2 T. unhulled sesame seeds
1 T. sesame oil
1 T. canola oil
4 T. water
Extra all-purpose flour for rolling

1. Blend together all-purpose flour, brown rice flour, salt, and sesame seeds.
2. Add two kinds of oil and water to flour mixture.
3. Blend wet ingredients into dry ingredients until a soft dough is formed.
4. Sprinkle rolling surface with all-purpose flour and roll dough to ⅛-inch thickness.
5. Cut into 2-inch circles.
6. Place circles on ungreased cookie sheets.
7. Re-form dough scraps into a ball, re-roll, and cut into circles until all dough is used.
8. Prick each circle two or three times with the tines of a fork.
9. Bake until golden brown on the bottom.

Soda Crackers

A simple, old-fashioned recipe good with soups, for upset stomachs, or with just about any dip or spread.

YIELD: APPROXIMATELY 30–36 2-INCH CIRCLES
BAKE: 350° FOR 15–18 MINUTES OR UNTIL GOLDEN BROWN ON BOTTOM

1¼ C. unbleached all-purpose flour
½ tsp. salt
1 tsp. baking powder
2 T. canola oil
4 T. water
Extra all-purpose flour for rolling
Extra salt to sprinkle on top

1. Mix together all-purpose flour, salt, and baking powder.
2. Add canola oil and water.
3. Blend wet ingredients into dry ones until a smooth dough is formed.
4. Sprinkle flat surface with all-purpose flour and roll dough to ⅛-inch thickness.
5. Cut dough into 2-inch circles.
6. Place circles on ungreased cookie sheets.
7. Re-form dough scraps into a ball, re-roll, and cut into circles until all dough is used.
8. Prick circles two or three times with the tines of a fork.
9. Sprinkle tops with extra salt, if desired.
10. Bake until golden brown on the bottom.

Note: Because these crackers contain baking powder, they will be slightly puffy once baked.

Tequila and Key Lime Crackers

Blend your favorite tequila with key lime in this cracker. Great served with homemade salsa with a margarita on the side.

YIELD: APPROXIMATELY 24–26 2-INCH CIRCLES
BAKE: 350° FOR 15–18 MINUTES OR UNTIL GOLDEN BROWN ON BOTTOM

1¼ C. unbleached all-purpose flour
½ tsp. salt
2 T. canola oil
2 T. fresh key lime juice (about 2 limes)
2 T. favorite tequila
Extra all-purpose flour for rolling

1. Mix together all-purpose flour and salt.
2. Add canola oil, lime juice, and tequila.
3. Blend wet ingredients into dry ingredients until a soft dough is formed.
4. Sprinkle rolling area with all-purpose flour and roll dough to ⅛-inch thickness.
5. Cut dough into 2-inch circles.
6. Place circles on ungreased cookie sheets.
7. Re-form dough scraps into a ball, re-roll, and cut into circles until all dough is used.
8. Prick each circle two or three times with the tines of a fork.
9. Bake until golden brown on the bottom.

Toasted Wheat Germ and Mace Crackers

Nutty, crunchy wheat germ forms the base of this mace-flavored cracker.

YIELD: Approximately 28–30 2-inch circles
BAKE: 350° for 15–18 minutes or until golden brown on bottom

¾ C. toasted wheat germ (use pre-toasted or toast your own)
¾ C. unbleached all-purpose flour
½ tsp. salt
1 tsp. mace powder
2 T. canola oil
4 T. water
Extra all-purpose flour for rolling

1. Mix together wheat germ, all-purpose flour, salt, and mace.
2. Add canola oil and water.
3. Blend wet ingredients into dry ingredients until a soft dough is formed.
4. Sprinkle rolling area with all-purpose flour and roll dough to ⅛-inch thickness.
5. Cut dough into 2-inch circles.
6. Place circles on ungreased cookie sheets.
7. Re-form dough scraps into a ball, re-roll, and cut into circles until all dough is used.
8. Prick each circle two or three times with the tines of a fork.
9. Bake until golden brown on the bottom.

Tomato and Basil Crackers

Similar to a mini pizza, this cracker has a rich tomato flavor and a wonderful reddish tint to it.

YIELD: APPROXIMATELY 30–36 2-INCH CIRCLES
BAKE: 350° FOR 15–18 MINUTES OR UNTIL LIGHT BROWN ON BOTTOM

1¼ C. unbleached all-purpose flour
½ tsp. salt
1–1½ tsp. dried basil
4 T. water
2 T. tomato paste
2 T. olive oil
Extra all-purpose flour for rolling

1. Mix together flour, salt, and basil.
2. Add water, tomato paste, and oil.
3. Blend wet ingredients into dry ingredients until a soft dough is formed.
4. Sprinkle rolling area with all-purpose flour and roll dough to ⅛-inch thickness.
5. Cut dough into 2-inch circles.
6. Place circles on ungreased cookie sheets.
7. Re-form dough scraps into a ball, re-roll, and cut into circles until all dough is used.
8. Prick each circle two or three times with the tines of a fork.
9. Bake until golden brown on the bottom.

Whole Wheat Crackers

The nutty flavor of whole wheat with a slightly sweet aftertaste.

YIELD: APPROXIMATELY 30–36 2-INCH CIRCLES
BAKE: 350° FOR 15–18 MINUTES OR UNTIL GOLDEN BROWN ON BOTTOM

1 C. whole wheat flour
¼ C. unbleached all-purpose flour
½ tsp. salt
1 tsp. sugar
2 T. olive oil
4 T. water
Extra all-purpose flour for rolling

1. Blend together whole wheat and all-purpose flours, salt, and sugar.
2. Add olive oil and water.
3. Blend wet ingredients into dry ingredients until a soft dough is formed.
4. Sprinkle rolling area with all-purpose flour and roll dough to ⅛-inch thickness.
5. Cut dough into 2-inch circles.
6. Place circles on ungreased cookie sheets.
7. Re-form dough scraps into a ball, re-roll, and cut into circles until all dough is used.
8. Prick each circle two or three times with the tines of a fork.
9. Bake until golden brown on the bottom.

Whole Wheat Peanut Butter Crackers

Smooth or crunchy peanut butter blends well with whole wheat in these savory crackers, great with a dab of jelly on top.

YIELD: APPROXIMATELY 30–36 2-INCH CRACKERS
BAKE: 350° FOR 15–20 MINUTES OR UNTIL GOLDEN BROWN ON BOTTOM

¾ C. whole wheat flour
½ C. unbleached all-purpose flour
½ tsp. salt
½ C. smooth or crunchy peanut butter
5–6 T. water
Extra all-purpose flour for rolling

1. Blend together whole wheat and all-purpose flours, and salt.
2. Add peanut butter and water.
3. Blend wet ingredients into dry ingredients until a smooth dough is formed. If dough is too dry, add a few drops more water.
4. Sprinkle rolling area with all-purpose flour and roll dough to ⅛- to ¼-inch thickness. Dough is dense, so rolling to proper thinness may require some extra pressure.
5. Cut dough into 2-inch circles.
6. Place circles on ungreased cookie sheets.
7. Re-form dough scraps into a ball, re-roll, and cut into circles until all dough is used.
8. Prick each circle two or three times with the tines of a fork.
9. Bake until golden brown on the bottom.

DIPS AND SPREADS

SOME THOUGHTS ON DIPS AND SPREADS

NOW THAT YOU HAVE A WIDE ASSORTMENT OF CRACKERS and you've eaten plenty of them plain, it's time to make some homemade dips and spreads to go with them. Nothing beats a homemade cracker spread with Curried Egg Spread or dipped into some fresh Tomato Salsa. One of my favorite pastimes is to make a variety of dips and spreads and invite a few friends over for a wine and hors d'oeuvre party. I bake three or four kinds of crackers, whip up five or six types of dips and spreads, add a couple blocks of cheese, a few bottles of wine, place some good music in the CD player, and then sit back and enjoy the fun.

I've included just a few ideas to get you started, hoping many of you will take these ideas and experiment, just as you've done with the crackers. All the following recipes can be doubled or tripled to increase the yields or use the listed amounts and make more types of dips for an assortment of flavors. And try combining spreads on a cracker, such as the Cucumber and Dill Spread topped with the Cilantro and Lime Spread.

Enjoy!

Artichoke Heart Spread

A mild spread that's nice in the springtime. Add a few red pepper flakes for a little more zip.

YIELD: Approx. 1 C.

1 can (14 oz.) artichoke hearts in water, drained
2 T. olive oil
1 tsp. Italian seasoning
¼ tsp. salt

Place all ingredients in a food processor and blend until smooth. Given the nature of artichoke hearts, there will be some bits and pieces still visible in the dip.

If you prefer, you can use the marinated artichoke hearts found in a jar, but those have been marinated in soybean and other, less desirable oils and may not be as flavorful as making your own.

GOES WITH:

Carrot and Ginger Crackers
Soda Crackers

Basil Spread

The quintessential summer spread, my own variation of pesto.

YIELD: Approx. ⅓ C.

1 C. fresh basil leaves, loosely packed
2 T. olive oil
⅛ tsp. salt
2 T. ground walnuts

Place all ingredients in a food processor and blend until smooth. I used walnuts instead of pine nuts and did not add Parmesan, but these may be added for a more traditional pesto.

Other greens such as arugula may be substituted for the basil to make a different-flavored spread.

GOES WITH:
Cheddar Cheese Crackers
Multi-Grain Crackers

Black Bean Dip

Soft and creamy, this dip is a hit with kids and adults alike.

YIELD: Approx. 1 C.

1 15 oz. can black beans, drained
¾ tsp. cumin
½ tsp. chili powder
¼ tsp. onion powder
¼ tsp. salt

Place all ingredients in a food processor and blend until smooth.

GOES WITH:

Mole Crackers
Salsa and Cornmeal Crackers

Black Olive Spread

Salty and creamy, this spread is my variation of a tapenade.

YIELD: Approx. ½ C.

½ can (net wt.dr. 6 oz) small black olives, drained
2 T. olive oil
⅛ tsp. garlic salt
½ tsp. apple cider vinegar

Place all ingredients in a food processor and blend until smooth.

GOES WITH:

Onion Lover's Cracker
Rosemary Crackers

Cilantro and Lime Spread

Tangy and spicy, either you love cilantro or you hate it.

YIELD: Approx. ¼ C.

1 C. loosely packed cilantro leaves (some stems are okay)
1 T. olive oil
½ key lime, juiced
Pinch of salt

Place all ingredients in a food processor and blend until smooth.

GOES WITH:

Bacon Crackers
Tequila and Key Lime Crackers

Corn and Sweet Relish Spread

Sweet, creamy, and refreshing.

YIELD: Approx. ¾ C.

1 C. frozen corn, thawed
1 T. olive oil
1½ tsp. sweet relish
⅛ tsp. salt

Place all ingredients in a food processor and blend until smooth.

GOES WITH:

Almond Lover's Cracker
Carrot and Millet

Cucumber and Dill Spread

A perky flavor combination that's cooling and energizing.

YIELD: Approx. ½ C.

½ cucumber, peeled, seeds removed
½ tsp. dried dill
Pinch of salt
1 T. olive oil

Place all ingredients in a food processor and blend until smooth. Drain off any extra water that might appear after the cucumbers have sweated due to the salt in spread.

GOES WITH:

Lemon and Dill Crackers
Whole Wheat Crackers

Curried Egg Spread

The spicy taste of curry blended with the mild flavor of eggs…yum!

YIELD: Approx. ½ C.

2 large eggs, hard-boiled, cooled, and peeled
1 T. olive oil
2 tsp. lemon juice
¼ tsp. salt
½ tsp. curry powder

Place all ingredients in a food processor and blend until smooth. You can also place all ingredients in a small bowl and mash thoroughly with a fork.

GOES WITH:

Curry and Brown Rice Crackers
Potato and Rye Crackers

Green Olive and Caper Spread

Briny and vinegary, great with a martini!

YIELD: Approx. ½ C.

½ C. green olives with pimientos
2 rounded tsp. capers
1 tsp. olive oil

Place all ingredients in a food processor and blend until smooth.

GOES WITH:

Oatmeal Crackers
Toasted Wheat Germ and Mace Crackers

Guacamole Dip

A version of this classic appetizer that I learned while living in Mexico.

YIELD: Approx. ¾ C.

1 ripe avocado, remove peel and pit
2 T. lemon juice or 2 key limes, juiced
⅛–¼ tsp. salt
½ tsp. cumin

Place all ingredients in a food processor and blend until smooth. Or you can mash the ingredients together in a bowl with a fork for a chunkier consistency.

GOES WITH:
Blue Cornmeal and Red Pepper Crackers
Hungarian Paprika and Cornmeal Crackers

Mushroom Spread

Great with a slice of cheddar cheese.

YIELD: Approx. ½ C.

6 button mushrooms, cut into quarters or eighths
½ tsp. Italian seasoning
¼ tsp. garlic salt *or* ½ clove garlic, finely chopped,
    with a pinch of salt
2 T. olive oil

Place all ingredients in a food processor and blend until smooth. Best if flavors are allowed to blend for an hour before serving.

GOES WITH:

Black Olive Crackers
Caraway and Rye Crackers

Mint Spread

The stimulating taste of mint in a slightly sweet spread.
Also great on ice cream.

YIELD: Approx. ¼ C.

1 C. fresh mint leaves, loosely packed
1–2 T. canola oil
1 T. sugar
¼–½ tsp. water

Place all ingredients in a food processor and blend until smooth.

GOES WITH:

Mint Crackers
Sesame Seed and Brown Rice Crackers

Pecan Butter Spread

A buttery-nutty variation on homemade peanut butter.

YIELD: Approx. 1 C.

1 C. pecan nuts
2 T. olive oil

Place all ingredients in a food processor and blend until smooth. Other nuts may be substituted for the pecans, such as almonds or hazelnuts. If using peanuts, reduce the amount of olive oil used or omit entirely.

GOES WITH:

Dried Cranberry and Graham Crackers
Orange and Buckwheat Crackers

Tomato Salsa

Best made with tomatoes fresh from the garden, a lovely reminder of summer.

YIELD: Approx. ¾ C.

2 fresh plum tomatoes
⅛ white onion
½ tsp. chili powder
½ tsp. cumin powder
¼ tsp. salt
½ key lime, juiced

Combine all ingredients in a food processor and blend until smooth. Several sprigs of cilantro may be added for those who like this herb. Increase the chili if you want a spicier salsa.

GOES WITH:

Guacamole Crackers
Tomato and Basil Crackers

White Bean and Chive Dip

A creamy dip full of the snappy onion flavor of chives.

YIELD: Approx. 1 C.

1 15 oz. can white beans, drained
6–8 fresh chives, chopped into pieces
⅜ tsp. salt
⅛ tsp. black pepper

Place all ingredients in a food processor and blend until smooth.

GOES WITH:

Balsamic Vinegar and Brown Rice Crackers
Beer and Rye Crackers

SOME THOUGHTS ON CHEESE

WHAT GOES BETTER WITH CRACKERS THAN CHEESE? Not much. But determining which type of cheese would go well with which cracker can be a bit confusing. Here's a good rule of thumb: The stronger the cracker flavor, the lighter the cheese flavor (and vice versa), so that the flavors don't mask each other. Of course, many people may prefer a stronger cheese flavor with a richer, spicier cracker, so the flavors balance each other. And again, the reverse is true as well; a mild cracker would do well with a mild cheese. In the end, it really comes down to experimentation and personal preference. Frankly, cheddar seems to go with just about anything. But here are some helpful places to start.

Brie: Rosemary Crackers, Tomato and Basil Crackers, Caraway and Rye Crackers, Orange and Buckwheat Crackers

Cheddar: Barbecue Crackers, Beer and Rye Crackers, Onion Lover's Crackers

Gouda: Cardamom and Whole Wheat Crackers, Honey and Thyme Crackers, Pistachio Crackers, Rosewater Crackers

Goat cheese: Carrot and Ginger Crackers, Green Tea and Brown Rice Crackers

Gruyère: Lemon and Poppy Seed Crackers, Maple and Sage Crackers

Monterey Jack: Tequila and Key Lime Crackers

Feel free to play around with favorite cheese and cracker combinations and remember to take notes on what tastes good to you.

ACKNOWLEDGMENTS

This book would not have been possible without my husband, Jeffrey Thomas, who acted as my chief taste tester for all these recipes. He willingly ate batch after trial batch of crackers and offered me fair criticism on each new version. He suggested refinements to each recipe so that every cracker would be a balance of taste and texture. Imagine my dismay when Jeffrey came down with a head cold and was unable to taste anything for over two weeks, right when I was in the middle of experimenting with the most recipes!

I'd also like to thank my two younger sons, Johann and Finn, who also acted as guinea pigs in this project and ate many a cracker. They even coerced their friends into trying some of the more unusual combinations, which was a big help to me. And my oldest son, Yule, provided encouragement over the phone from his island home of Hawaii.

My sincere gratitude to my mother, Joan Cart, who did all the illustrations. On somewhat short notice, she was able to provide an artistic layer to this book, a concept I had not even considered when I first started experimenting in the kitchen. And thanks to my dad, who always believes I am able to achieve whatever I set my mind to doing.

Big thanks are also due to my next-door neighbors, Angela DeRosa, Lucy Cayard, and Steve Cayard. Angela is an excellent cook in her own right, so her evaluation of flavors and suggestions for ways to tweak these recipes was a great help. Lucy's enthusiasm for the project helped me through many a dreary day when I thought I might be on the wrong track. And Steve provided a much-needed male perspective that was not overshadowed by being my spouse.

Amber Reed, a talented cook and cheesemaker, gave me the valuable insights on cheeses. I am grateful for Amber's help in this department.

Thanks to Martha Young and Richard Garrett for working with me on short notice on a muddy, snowy March day. It was good fun!

Other friends unknowingly played a part in this project by eating new cracker recipes at many potlucks and dinner parties. Usually known for my cookies, I brought trays of crackers to these gatherings instead, much to the dismay of some people hoping for my mint chocolate chip cookies. But I am thankful for the feedback I received from these folks as well.

And many, many thanks to Peter Burford, my editor at Burford Books, as well as all the other folks at Burford Books. Without Peter's feedback and encouragement, this project would probably never have been finished. Peter, many thanks for helping me fulfill one of my life dreams of writing my very own cookbook.

And thanks to you, dear reader—may you enjoy these recipes and have fun experimenting with flavors and ideas of your very own.

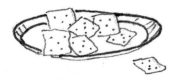